Hand-Stitched Heart

Regan Troop

BookLeaf Publishing

Presentation by *BookLeaf Publishing*

Web: www.bookleafpub.com

E-mail: info@bookleafpub.com

ISBN: 9782780531066

First edition 2022

DEDICATION

These works of poetry have been pulled from my heart for the heart of the reader,

You.

I don't know what you've lived through up until this moment, but I welcome you with strength and wisdom to continue living through your moments in Life. Feel them. Learn from them. Grow and flourish into an amazing, strong, beautiful you.

This book is also dedicated to the one who holds my heart ever so dearly. He knows of all its healed bruises and blue hues and is to blame for the warm bright reds. He is my best friend, my rock, my lover, the amazing father of our miraculous son, Connor. I am thankful for his everlasting support of my creative ambitions. Thank you, Nick Lightfoot, for this life of love you have given me.

ACKNOWLEDGEMENT

I would like to acknowledge all of the moments I've lived through that are reflected within these pages and their emotions, thoughts and teachings. Altogether they have evolved into these written works that I do hold dear to my hand-stitched heart. I can visit these pages any time. When I want to reminisce. When I want to look back at how far I've come as a human and as a writer. When I want to read through them after hearing from someone who was really touched by my words. I hope this book finds those who need it.

I would also like to thank BookLeaf Publishing for the amazing opportunity they gave me and so many other incredible writers worldwide. The creative process and outcome have been very rewarding all on their own. Thank you for making it possible to share the outcome of my hard work with others. I am proud yet I remain humbled to have been deemed worthy of publishing. This fuels my fire for writing new and improved works.

PREFACE

The words found within these pages are for the empaths, the healers, the ones who feel too deeply, the ones whose hearts and minds need mending of their own. This is my personal patchwork of hope and strength. Take my hand, come on in.

Inner Wild to Outer World

Whichever Wild rests within my body,
She has gleaming carnivorous teeth
and strong claws to grab a tight hold.

She's pacing restlessly and
isn't going to wait any longer.

Prepare yourself for
the sharp, the gripping and the bold.

Your Light Home

I'll be your light
for as long as it takes you to defeat your demons
of night
and find your way home to me.

I know it won't be tonight
because your demons they grip your every bone
with such might,
you break away but they pull you back in their
dark seas.

Find your way home to me please

because my hand is being dripped on by wax,
my light here is fading, and the darkness will
cover your tracks
then we'll both be lost and longing in their dark
seas.

My candle streams smoke,
I hold out my hand for you and I feel a tight
squeeze.
Is it you or your demons, who's grabbing at me?

Then I awoke.

You're right next to me.
Neither of us spoke, we just hugged,

and we breathed.

Real and Deep

the Pain is
real and deep

because so was
the Love.

Darlin'

Lipstick on her shot glass,
she warms her confidence with something sweet.
Beer wafted from the town jackass,
he tries his luck and swigs through
the greet,
"Dan's the name, and who might
you be, sweet girl?"

Last weekend he was John. Before then,
Earl.

"Guess my name," her ego sparks back to the
man she had met as John,
"It starts with a 'D'."
"Danielle! Darleen... Darcy?"

If he weren't so wasted there'd be no
questioning such a radiant lady.

"None of those." she lies. Embarrassment
fueling her red cheeks.

I can see through her eyes; she's stuffing her
heart away.

Last time they walked out, "I'll never forget
a girl like you", didn't he say?
This time instead,

"Well, I'll just call you Darlin'. Tell
me you're not already a wife?"
"I own a shop and live out of town." fired up,
she described her cousins life.
"Now isn't that something *hic*,
tell me more at my place?"

She smiled and paid me for her drink, and
stood up with a blazing grace,

"Not if you can't remember a girl like me" heels
scorching out of his space.

Whispering Weapon

Did it hurt?
When your heart caved in and turned a deep hue
from tormenting visions of her round hips
as his grin grew?

Did it hurt?
When the sweet whisper of “I still love you”
from her soft, lingering, traitorous lips
touched your skin, too?

Did it hurt?
When your "crazy" mind actually knew
from the shade of red on her fingertips
"Deadly Sin Screw"?

Did it hurt?
When she threw all your love away for spew,
from within you chose to come to grips
with a brighter future in view.

Coffee-Stained Letter

Three knocks echoed through my home.
An envelope had arrived outside my door.
It read on the back, the ink dark blue,

"Everything that
I could never tell you"

My hands tremble,
this is nerving yet exciting.
Slowly raising the paper,
I recognize the handwriting.

"I was going to send one of those bouquets
that come with a small card,
but my words won't fit on a throwaway
and I didn't want to catch you off guard.
I thought about visiting you,
to explain myself, but I knew
I rushed into things before
when I gave into my desire to say
“I can see my life with you in it, every day.”
I miss you more than I can write;
I can't enjoy our Coffee Talks that once
filled this household; your cup always sits cold.
I can't find my comfy spot at night

where it was my arms wrapped around you tight.
I wouldn't want anyone else
who might try to make me smile.
There's so much more I need to say
if you'll listen to me for a while.
I'll take things as slowly as needed, my patience
has been reformed.
I'm in the coffee shop across from your place
keeping your cup warm."

My hands softened,
absorbing the coffee-stained letter.
Slowly raising the paper,
to my heart beneath his sweater.

I rush out the door
after reading his last line in blue.
Realizing the same feeling deep in my core,
"I Love You."

Undersea

Just like the crashing waves,
I can't stop my feelings
that collide for you.
So instead
I take the plunge,
immersed in your undersea,
hoping you don't
let me sink.

Memory Etched in Ember

I walked through the public park
during the chilly Autumn season.
Leaves were falling, the color of monarchs,
like they hardly needed a reason.

A little warmth had greeted me on the park
bench,
probably from the elder woman with the suede
gloves.
She always sat here with birdseed clenched
to feed the sparrows and the doves.

For a while I admired the melting sky,
the gardens and the silhouetting trees.
A friendly stranger waved on by,
His identity a blur to me.

A leaf had landed beside me, it twirled around
amused.
Celebrating in dance the full cycle of its lifetime.
I got caught up in the moment, mind twirled
around confused.
Questioning why I decided to sit here, every
time.

A gust had taken my waltzing friend,
which whisked my eyes to letters carved in wood.
I had to squint, then over I had to bend,
"Stay etched in my heart forever, if you could".

A second stranger spoke my name,
In my heart, his voice rekindled an ember.
He had the same smile as my old flame,
The one I swore I'd always remember.

He reached out with a warm aged hand
until it met my suede glove, then I understood.
I told him of the bench carver's plan,
He smiled,
"And she said she would".

To be Loved by You

You pulled my heartstrings
for so long
that when they finally detached
from my aching heart,
so did I detach
from all emotions.

This is how it was
to be loved by you.

To be dead cold and empty
in the end.

Flawless

When it comes to Despondency,
It doesn't matter if you're standing
in its light cloudy mist
or in its heavy torrential downpour;
You will get wet.

Please find something warm
to give you solace
because you are human; we all make mistakes.
And by that definition, my dear,
you are flawless.

Smelling Roses

"You gon'a sleep all mornin', Bud?"

We get up for our day.
Breakfast first, or else we're both wild animals.
He walks over in such a way,
An older version of my loyal pal.

A gentle soul,
A trusted friend.
He makes me whole,
He's a tired old ten.

"You stop to smell the roses, Bud?"

He lays down,
Breathless, aching body,
But oh man that was a great walk.
His smile can't be turned into a frown.

A restful soul,
Last night I lost my best friend.
In my heart, a sunken hole,
At least now I won't have to pretend.

"You just sleep in now, Bud."

To Those who have Betrayed Me

To those who have betrayed me,
there's no coming back from what you've done.
Although I can only try to understand for the
sake of my sanity,
understand that I had to put you to the run.

I do not forgive treason so it's best you have
fallen back.
The loyalty between us exists no more
and you no longer have my back,
So, the ties have been severed like a cord.

The truth has chased you out of my life
like flaming arrows storming your route.
They've torched the bridge to end this strife,
your exile is absolute.

I do not value those who no longer value me.
I've carved you out of my stoic heart with ease
and fed you to the wolves.

As you now walk your path of faithlessness,
I stand here feeling in my heart a
courageousness.

If you ever make the mistake of coming back to
me
the only warmth there will be,
will be flaming arrows and hot-breathed wolves.

Flame to Ash to Flame

Searing Words
Allegations
I've been hunted for generations

Self-Destructive Habits
Charcoal Dark Thoughts
The abuse I've endured has been lots

Flame
to Ash
Burning me alive was their backlash

Ember
to Spark
They didn't know I always rise from the dark

Soul Rebirth
Brilliant Flame
I'll give you reasons to remember my name

Soar
above all doubts and win this war

The Mountains

You can have my heart
but my soul will always belong to the
mountains.
One day when my spirit departs,
to the highest winds it will be surmounting.

So, if you ever come to need me,
Bring my burned bones to the highlands.
Call my name from amongst the spruce trees,
and offer me a warm drink for us to unify hands.

Share with me grand tales of your successes.
You can have the last sip for your losses.
Now I must share something about your stresses,
so, rest your head down where the moss is.

Gaze upon their sun-kissed ridges everlasting.
The arise of life's problems may too, seem
unending.
But you can shine above any obstacle
forecasting,
if you just simply start climbing towards their
mending.

You have always held the biggest piece of my
heart,
My son, you are my light, and I am
so proud of you.
Know that we are never too far apart
as I rejoin the highest winds, I love you.

Return to the Wild Sea

Drowning her lips
in a warm cup of dark tea,
she listens closely to her memory
of the wild sea.
One day soon, she will return.
She will return home
to drown her lips
in the salty sea.

Drift Away

I still think of you,

In the way the winter wind is bitter cold
and steals the breath from my lungs
for just one second
before I catch my breath again.

Let it be known to you,

That's how barely detectable
your existence is in my mind.
These last cold bitter words of you
drift away with the wind, too.

Abandonment

At a time when I needed you the most,
your unconditional love for me became
conditional.
It was then I realized something had changed
and you became host
to something apathetic, selfish and oppositional.

I feel like you left me
and allowed some stranger to take your place.
Some stranger who doesn't care to know me
but expects me to act like he created time and
space.

He momentarily hears but won't listen to what
I'm saying,
there's an impatience and hidden agenda lurking
behind his eyes.
They haven't brought you back, the many moons
I've been praying,
for every next morning it's the same stranger
who continues to rise.

There's much more that I could go on to say
but what does it matter if you'll never return one
day?

My mind has been marked by fraught,
I always imagined our goodbye would be in death,
but it was not.
It was in abandonment.

Licking Wounds

When you ditched a puppy and ignored its cries
then finally answered it with,
"I don't need you in my life"

***

Now your ways of the past you do agnize
and you jab yourself, because of this strife,
with a poisoned arrow dipped in Regret.
The friendship we had, you cannot reclaim
and I won't come back when you call out my
name.

I won't be the one to lick your wounds
when I healed mine, alone, by light of many
moons.

I am Woman. I am Warrior.

I am self-respectful because
I was completely selfless and taken advantage of
I am courageous because
I was scared but stood my ground anyway
I am warmhearted because
I was lonely being brokenhearted
I am wise because
I was naïve but learned from many of
my mistakes
I am my own hero because
I was the only one who could
save me

I am a warrior because
I will always fight;
for myself, for my family,
for what's right and what's
good

Hand-Stitched Hearts

She has a selflessness nature in her soft hands
that never point a finger in demand.
She has a comforting embrace
to keep wild emotions in place.
I long for them to wrap around my space.

She has a backbone she worked hard for.
No one walks over her anymore
yet she remains kind in her candor.
She has a wondrously attractive mind
whose mysteries keep me in spellbind.
Oh, the inner workings of womankind.

She has a warm smile
melting anything hostile,
although it glows for only awhile.
She has full luscious lips
that anxiety bites off strips.

She has windblown hair
falling on shoulders bare.
Days like these she covers under a blanket of
self-care.
She has lovely legs revealing
her weakened state through their kneeling.

She's a healer in need of healing.

She has eyes that shine through the dark
and a hand-stitched heart.
I've learned to appreciate beautiful art.

She is my sister, my mother, my best friend,
She is the loving one with a heart to mend.
she is they, she is you, she is I,
She is as many of us as there are stars in the sky.

Lake Nymphs' Healing Chant

Water still and clear as glass
Ripple around my tiptoes at last
Swallow my legs, thighs and hips
Sip over my curves and up to my lips

Body of mine in this body of water
Recognize me as my ancestors' daughter
Flow through my spirit, mind and veins
Heal my bruises, aches and pains

I rest here weightless in this lake
Cured of my wounds and heartache
Body glistening in the suns rays
I tilt my gaze and give warm praise

Manufactured by Amazon.ca
Bolton, ON

24952427R00022